The
CRAFTY HANDS
Collection

Rag Dolls
Salt Dough Models
Simple Projects in Patchwork
Face Painting & Fancy Dress

First published in English in Great Britain
1995 by Aurum Press Ltd,
25 Bedford Avenue, London WC1B 3AT

Translated by Lydia Darbyshire

English translation copyright © Aurum Press 1995

First published as
Petits Modèles en Pâte à Sel
1988 by Éditions Fleurus,
11 rue Duguay-Trouin, 75006 Paris, France

Copyright © Éditions Fleurus 1988

A catalogue record for this book is available from the British Library

ISBN 1 85410 328 8

1 3 5 7 9 10 8 6 4 2
1995 1997 1999 1998 1996

Printed in Italy

The
CRAFTY HANDS
Collection

SALT DOUGH MODELS

Text, illustrations and modelling by
Catherine Baillaud
Photographs by Luc Bérujeau

To my helpers

Aurum Press

INTRODUCTION

Salt dough is the perfect medium for modelling. Just take some flour, add salt and water, and you have a smooth, malleable material to shape and bake into all kinds of long-lasting, three-dimensional objects.

If you want to make a special gift for a friend, some pretty table-decorations or simply a toy, then hurry to the kitchen and get out the flour and salt. The ingredients are readily obtainable, the method is simple, and the technique is easily learned.

Even small children can work with salt dough, and they can change and adapt the models shown here as they wish. Just see that they follow the basic technique, that the figures are neatly finished and that the joins are secure.

All the models described in this book can be air-dried rather than baked in the oven, which makes them especially safe for children to make. They will simply be less solid so, again, make sure that the joins are secure. Air-drying takes quite a long time, however, at least overnight, so it's not for the impatient.

However, the pieces will look better if you *do* bake your finished work before painting and varnishing it, and, because they are small, the figures shown on the pages that follow are easy to bake. Larger pieces are more likely to break up, and they take longer to cook. As long as you have the patience and dexterity to make them, tiny figures not only look much more appealing but can be cooked in next to no time.

So, cover your kitchen table with a waxed cloth and make sure you have some clean water nearby so that you can wash off the salt from your hands.

You can also make edible figures by modelling in marzipan or pastry. Practise with salt dough first, so that you can work with confidence in more difficult materials.

Salt dough is inedible, although, whether left in its natural state or coloured with vegetable dyes, it is not harmful – merely unpalatable. And for this reason it is an ideal material for children to play and model with.

Here – for the impatient, the imaginative, the generous – are ideas to stimulate your imagination and finished pieces that you can copy, all of which can be simply and quickly made. We show just a few of the many ways in which salt dough can be used to make amusing, attractive articles – fun to make and a pleasure to receive.

MATERIALS
AND EQUIPMENT

SALT

FLOUR

TABLE
SALT

PLAIN
FLOUR

KITCHEN FOIL
FOR COOKING

PAPER CLIPS

PLASTIC FILM
IN WHICH TO
WRAP THE
DOUGH SO
THAT IT
DOESNT DRY
OUT

PASTA—
SPAGHETTI
CANNELLONI
MACARONI

POINTED KNIFE

INKS,
PENS,
FELT-TIPPED
PENS

CRAYONS,
WATERCOLOURS,
CRAFT OR GOUACHE
PAINTS,
PAINTBRUSHES

A WIDE-
MOUTHED CONTAINER
IN WHICH TO PLUNGE
THE OBJECTS
TO VARNISH
THEM

CLEAR GLOSS
POLYURETHANE
VARNISH TO
PROTECT THE
MODELS FROM
DAMP

WATER

RECIPE

① USE 1 PART SALT TO 2 PARTS FLOUR AND SOME WATER

② MIX THE SALT WITH A LITTLE WATER— JUST ENOUGH TO DAMP IT

③ MIX IN THE FLOUR, AND THEN ADD SMALL AMOUNTS OF WATER

You need just three things – table salt, plain flour and water.

Salt

If you want a smooth, soft dough, use a good-quality table salt. Do not use sea salt because the crystals will be visible when you have finished, and if you are making large quantities the salt will hurt your hands.

Water

Be careful not to add too much water. You should add it little by little as you work. Aim for a dough that is firm and does not collapse and crumble when you shape it. If the dough is too soft, add more flour. Remember, you'll achieve the best results if you add the water drop by drop, mixing it in thoroughly each time.

Colouring

Watercolour and gouache paints, inks and even instant coffee can be used to colour the dough.

TEST TO SEE IF THE DOUGH IS THE RIGHT CONSISTENCY BY PLACING A MOUND ON THE TABLE. IF IT DOESN'T COLLAPSE, NEITHER WILL YOUR FIGURES.

MODELLING

Try to keep the dough clean, and, because it tends to dry out, you need to work as quickly and accurately as you can.

The success of a salt dough figure lies in the way you use a lot of small pieces to create one large model. It isn't a good idea to work with one large piece, as you might do with, say, clay. Salt dough figures that have been re-shaped and pulled about always look uneven and clumsily made. Also, they don't cook evenly and puff up in all the wrong places when they are baked.

If you are going to make a model of a face or a mask, for example, don't try to pull and push a large piece of dough into shape. You'll get far better results if you use lots of small pieces to build up the features, even though having to work in this way can seem tedious and unnecessary.

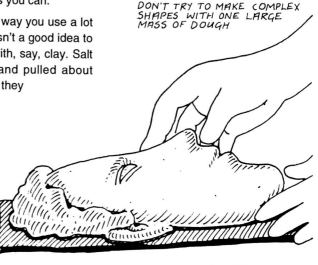

DON'T TRY TO MAKE COMPLEX SHAPES WITH ONE LARGE MASS OF DOUGH

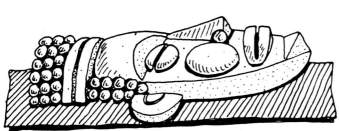

The larger the figure, the more individual pieces you will need to add, and this will increase the risk that the piece will not bake evenly and that it will be irregularly coloured.

When you make small pieces – less than about 4cm/1½in across – uneven puffing up during cooking isn't usually a serious problem, and it's possible to use your fingers to shape the pieces as you wish.

PREPARE THE VARIOUS PIECES YOU WILL NEED BEFORE YOU BEGIN

HOLD THE KNIFE UPRIGHT WHEN YOU WANT TO DRAW ON THE DOUGH, AND PRESS SUFFICIENTLY HARD...

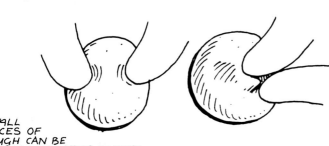

SMALL PIECES OF DOUGH CAN BE SHAPED WITH YOUR FINGERS

...TO MAKE A FAIRLY DEEP MARK

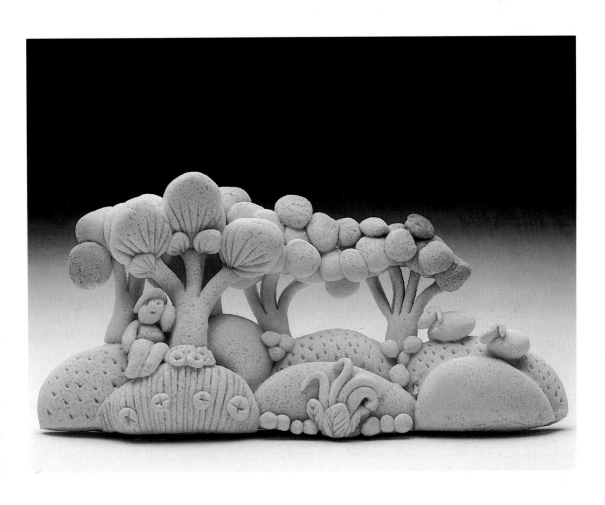

HOW MUCH TO USE?

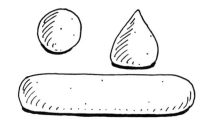

Pieces of dough that have been smoothed into little balls, rolled into sausages and strips, or rolled out and lightly folded will cook evenly. Try to avoid cutting out pieces with a knife so that the edges are absolutely smooth and flat, because it's difficult to predict how evenly they will bake.

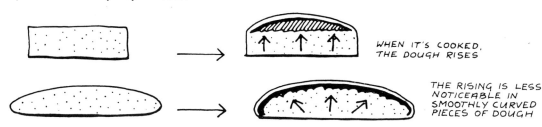

WHEN IT'S COOKED, THE DOUGH RISES

THE RISING IS LESS NOTICEABLE IN SMOOTHLY CURVED PIECES OF DOUGH

It's better to use a lot of small pieces that have limited surface areas. As soon as you have a large piece it is difficult to cook it properly – large pieces rise unevenly and often do not dry out thoroughly.

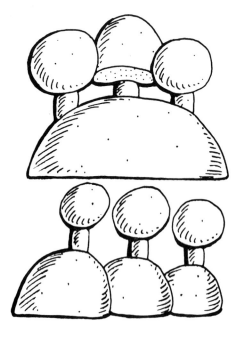

THE LARGER THE PIECE OF DOUGH, THE MORE LIKELY IT IS THAT THE SURFACE WILL BLISTER AND CRACK

HANGERS

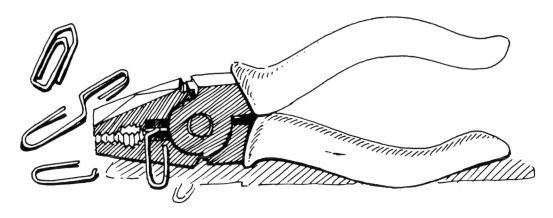

Paper clips are ideal. Open them out, cut them in two and insert in the dough before baking. They make very secure hangers.

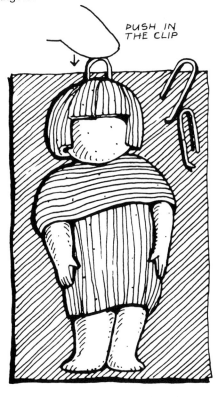

PUSH IN THE CLIP

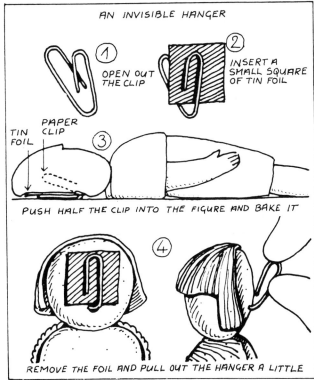

AN INVISIBLE HANGER

① OPEN OUT THE CLIP

② INSERT A SMALL SQUARE OF TIN FOIL

TIN FOIL   PAPER CLIP

③ PUSH HALF THE CLIP INTO THE FIGURE AND BAKE IT

④ REMOVE THE FOIL AND PULL OUT THE HANGER A LITTLE

COOKING OR DRYING?

BAKING THE FIGURES

If you let the dough dry out before baking it, you will not improve the appearance of the finished object. The surface of the dough will be covered in little holes and any pieces that are attached may become detached during baking. If you are making several items and want to cook them all at the same time, keep the finished ones protected under kitchen plastic film until you are ready.

All the models shown in this book were cooked at a temperature of 150°C/300°F/gas mark 2. The time needed for cooking depends on the size and number of items in the oven. The smaller the pieces are, the more quickly they will cook – and they will spoil if you leave them in too long, so keep an eye on them. Experiment with some practice pieces because ovens vary, and you may find that you need a lower temperature.

To save cooking time, take the figures off the tin foil as soon as the dough is fairly hard. Turn down the temperature and return them to the oven, handling as little as possible, until they are absolutely dry.

Before you paint and varnish the figure, make sure that the dough is absolutely dry. If the dough is the slightest bit damp, the paint and varnish will not adhere.

DRYING

If you decide to leave the figures to dry rather than cook them, make sure that you do not make the pieces too thick. Place the figures on kitchen paper (not foil).

1. If you have made your figures too thick, they will not dry

without cracking and shrinking. Don't try to make special pieces this way, because it isn't possible to make perfect balls and smooth edges.

2. On the other hand, flattened shapes are ideal for this process. The greater the surface area to be dried, the better will be the finished item. Don't try to smooth over cracks that appear during the drying process. You can get a pancake shape with smooth edges by flattening a ball of dough. If you want shapes with straight edges, cut them with a sharp knife.

3. You can make all kinds of shapes from flattened balls of dough, and they keep their shape well while they dry.

4. If you allow a fairly large flat rectangle or square to dry, the corners will tend to curl up as the dough dries. To overcome this, turn over the piece from time to time while it dries.

Attaching extra pieces

The advantage of air-drying a dough figure is that, unlike a baked piece, any pieces that have been joined on to the basic shape are less likely to become detached as the dough dries. When you make a figure that you intend to air-dry, you must take into account that the dough will shrink as it dries, so you must exaggerate each feature slightly.

Dampen the dough a little and make sure that the piece you are attaching is pressed firmly onto the main piece.

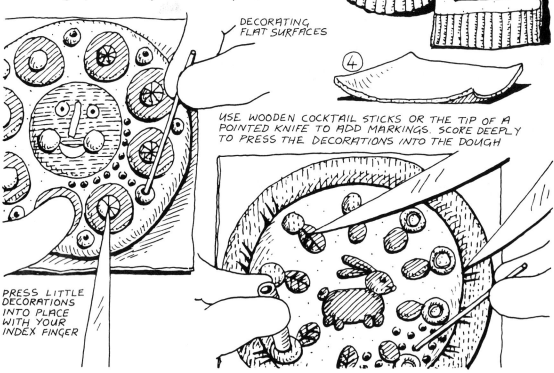

DECORATING FLAT SURFACES

USE WOODEN COCKTAIL STICKS OR THE TIP OF A POINTED KNIFE TO ADD MARKINGS. SCORE DEEPLY TO PRESS THE DECORATIONS INTO THE DOUGH

PRESS LITTLE DECORATIONS INTO PLACE WITH YOUR INDEX FINGER

Air-drying takes a long time. For that reason it's best to make small pieces and, in winter, to place them near a radiator to dry. Remember that air-dried salt dough is much more fragile than baked dough, so always be extra careful when you handle these items.

ADD FLATTENED CIRCLES OF DOUGH TO THE BODY. ROLL OVER AND OVER TO PRESS THEM INTO THE SURFACE

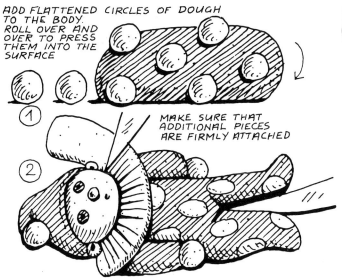

MAKE SURE THAT ADDITIONAL PIECES ARE FIRMLY ATTACHED

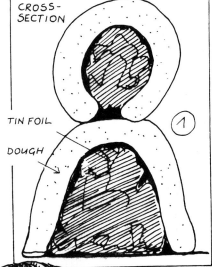

USE A PASTRY CUTTER OR SOME PASTA TO MAKE SMALL INDENTATIONS FOR THINGS LIKE EYES AND BUTTONS

CROSS-SECTION

TIN FOIL

DOUGH

Three-dimensional objects

If you want to make a piece in the round, you need to provide an internal framework if it's going to be more than about 3cm/1¼in high. Without a support, the piece will not dry properly. Screw some paper or pieces of foil into small balls and cover these with a sheet of dough, then add the details, making sure that the body of the finished piece is not too thick.

FLOWERS & PETALS

Salt dough is wonderful for modelling, but decoupage can be tricky. Cut-out dough has irregular outlines and the surface tends to puff up during baking. However, when individual petals and leaves are shaped and applied one by one around the edge, they will prevent the base from rising too much and also hold their own shape. To add petals and leaves, first model, then flatten them: the rounded shape won't puff up too much during cooking

For a wreath, add leaves around the edge of a circle, scoring the veins with the point of your knife and using the knife to press each leaf and petal firmly down onto the base.

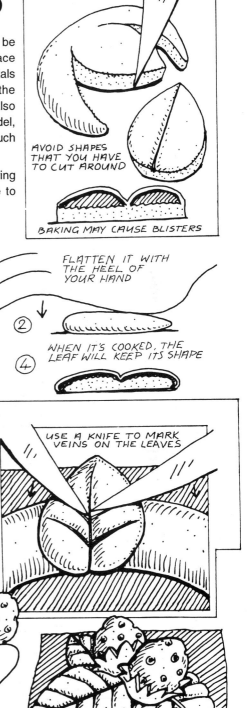

AVOID SHAPES THAT YOU HAVE TO CUT AROUND

BAKING MAY CAUSE BLISTERS

FLATTEN IT WITH THE HEEL OF YOUR HAND

① PULL A BALL INTO A PEAR-SHAPE

② WHEN IT'S COOKED, THE LEAF WILL KEEP ITS SHAPE

③ MARK THE CENTRAL VEIN

④

PRESS THE LEAF FIRMLY ONTO THE OUTSIDE CIRCLE WITH THE BLADE OF YOUR KNIFE

USE A KNIFE TO MARK VEINS ON THE LEAVES

PRACTISE MARKING THE SURFACE OF THE DOUGH WITHOUT TOUCHING IT WITH YOUR FINGERS

MAKE EACH PIECE SEPARATELY AND ATTACH THEM ONE AT A TIME

17

RIBBONS
AND BOWS

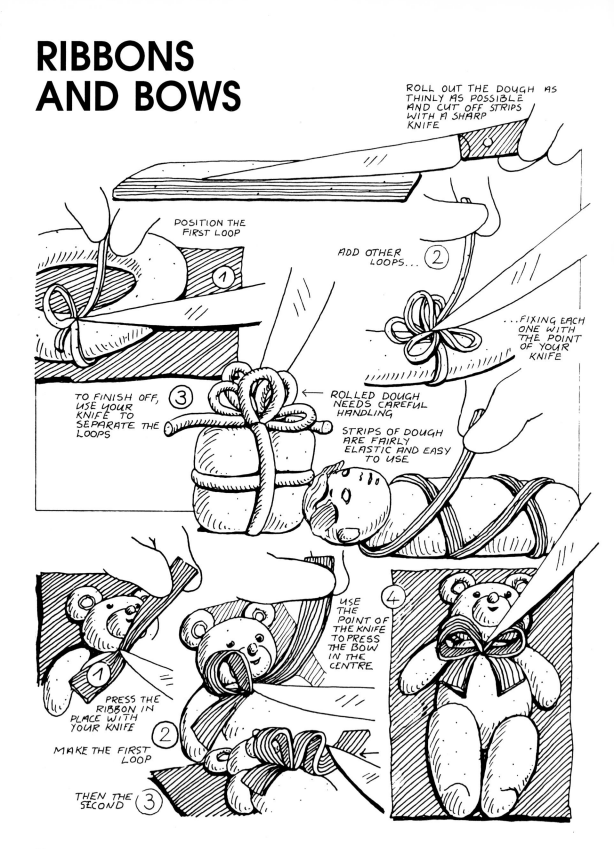

ROLL OUT THE DOUGH AS THINLY AS POSSIBLE AND CUT OFF STRIPS WITH A SHARP KNIFE

POSITION THE FIRST LOOP ①

ADD OTHER LOOPS... ②

...FIXING EACH ONE WITH THE POINT OF YOUR KNIFE

TO FINISH OFF, USE YOUR KNIFE TO SEPARATE THE LOOPS ③

← ROLLED DOUGH NEEDS CAREFUL HANDLING

STRIPS OF DOUGH ARE FAIRLY ELASTIC AND EASY TO USE

PRESS THE RIBBON IN PLACE WITH YOUR KNIFE ①

MAKE THE FIRST LOOP ②

THEN THE SECOND ③

USE THE POINT OF THE KNIFE TO PRESS THE BOW IN THE CENTRE ④

BASIC SHAPES

PREPARE ALL THE INDIVIDUAL PIECES

Begin with ball and sausage shapes. You will need to practise making smooth dough and forming it into neat shapes – a lot depends on the moisture content of the dough and the amount of pressure you exert as you knead and mould it.

USE DIFFERENT COLOURS

PUSH THEM INTO PLACE WITH YOUR INDEX FINGER

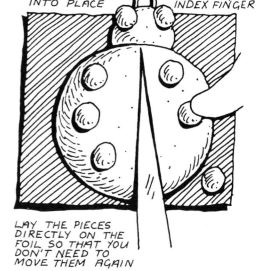

LAY THE PIECES DIRECTLY ON THE FOIL SO THAT YOU DON'T NEED TO MOVE THEM AGAIN

FOR BEST RESULTS, MAKE DEEP CUTS AND VERTICAL HOLES

MAKING IMPRESSIONS IN THE DOUGH HELPS THE PETALS STICK TO THE SURFACE

TO MAKE RAYS AND PETALS, HOLD THE KNIFE HORIZONTALLY AND SCORE THE DOUGH DEEPLY, FROM TOP TO BOTTOM, WITHOUT CUTTING RIGHT THROUGH

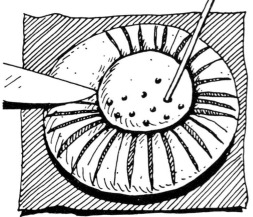

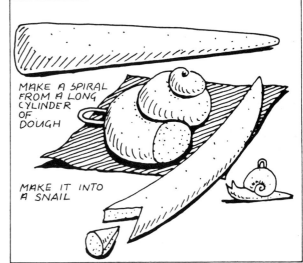

MAKE A SPIRAL FROM A LONG CYLINDER OF DOUGH

MAKE IT INTO A SNAIL

A DOUGH ROSE

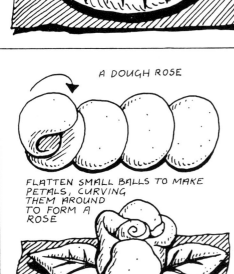

FLATTEN SMALL BALLS TO MAKE PETALS, CURVING THEM AROUND TO FORM A ROSE

REMOVE THE DOUGH FROM THE CENTRE OF A CONE, CUT AROUND THE TOP EDGE...

...AND FOLD BACK THE CUTS TO MAKE A FLOWER

FIGURES

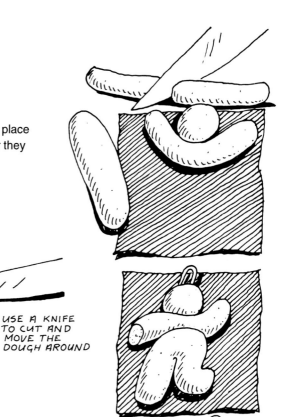

Make sure that you don't distort the pieces as you place them together and that they are firmly attached, or they will come apart in the oven.

USE A KNIFE TO CUT AND MOVE THE DOUGH AROUND

Decorate the figures with felt-tipped pens, ink or paints before applying a coat of varnish.

ANIMALS

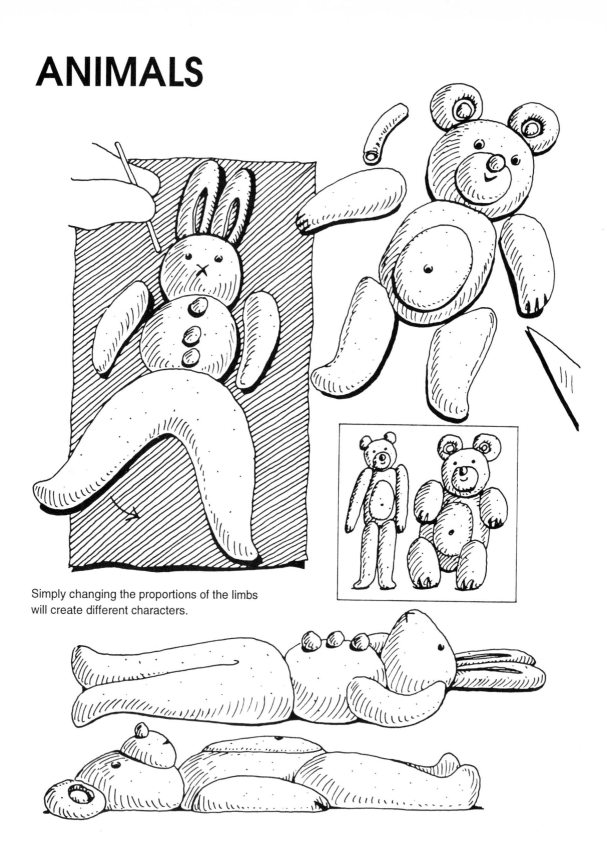

Simply changing the proportions of the limbs will create different characters.

THE PERFECT FINISH

Roll out the pieces in the palms of your hands or on a perfectly flat surface so that the dough is smooth before you decorate it with ink.

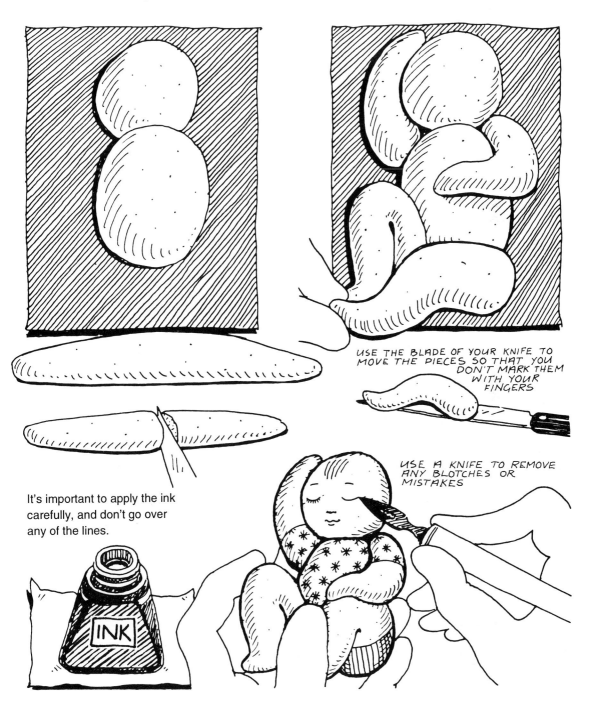

USE THE BLADE OF YOUR KNIFE TO MOVE THE PIECES SO THAT YOU DON'T MARK THEM WITH YOUR FINGERS

USE A KNIFE TO REMOVE ANY BLOTCHES OR MISTAKES

It's important to apply the ink carefully, and don't go over any of the lines.

INK

NUMBERS

Some of the most attractive pieces can be made from rolls of dough, bent into shape, and they don't blister when they are baked. You could use the same method to make letters of the alphabet and even to form entire words. Work fast so that the dough doesn't dry out before you bake it. The separate elements adhere better when the dough is moist.

FIGURINES

So that these little figures will stand upright, they need a fairly large base. If the base becomes mis-shapen in the oven, use a file, small saw or sharp knife to smooth the surface.

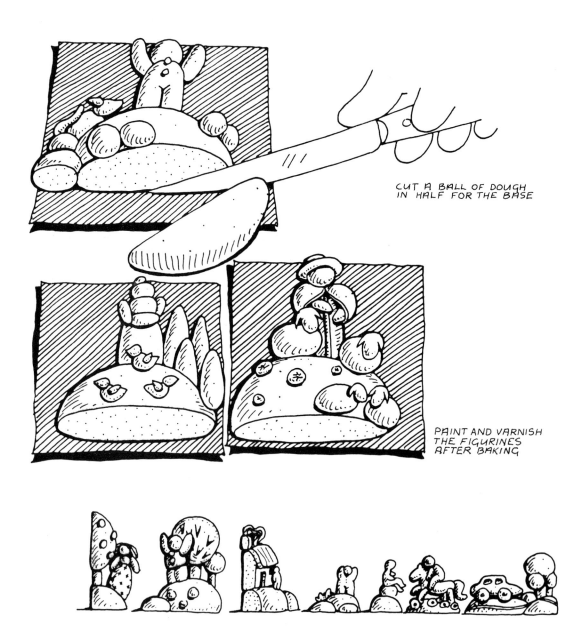

CUT A BALL OF DOUGH IN HALF FOR THE BASE

PAINT AND VARNISH THE FIGURINES AFTER BAKING

LITTLE PICTURES

To make them rigid, attach the figure in the centre to as many points on the frame as possible.

FAIRYTALE FIGURES

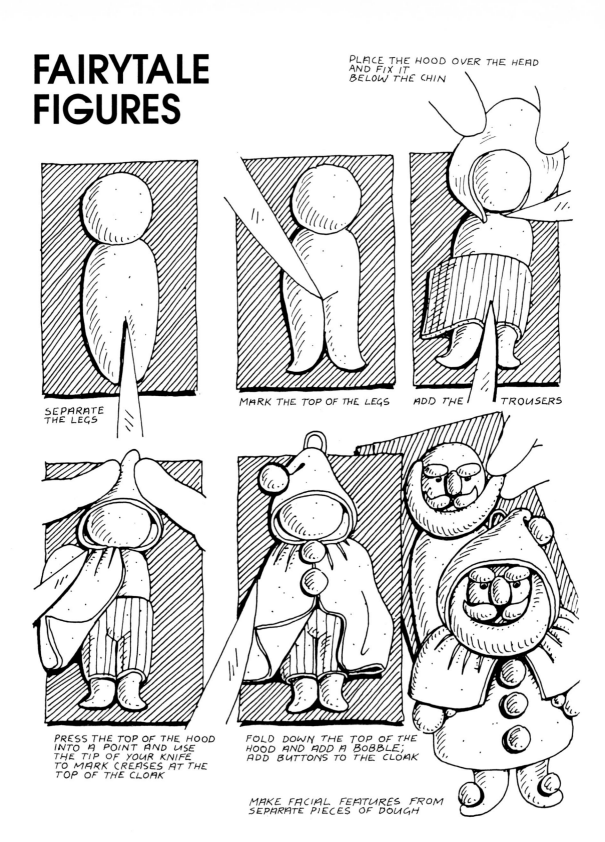

PLACE THE HOOD OVER THE HEAD AND FIX IT BELOW THE CHIN

SEPARATE THE LEGS

MARK THE TOP OF THE LEGS

ADD THE TROUSERS

PRESS THE TOP OF THE HOOD INTO A POINT AND USE THE TIP OF YOUR KNIFE TO MARK CREASES AT THE TOP OF THE CLOAK

FOLD DOWN THE TOP OF THE HOOD AND ADD A BOBBLE; ADD BUTTONS TO THE CLOAK

MAKE FACIAL FEATURES FROM SEPARATE PIECES OF DOUGH

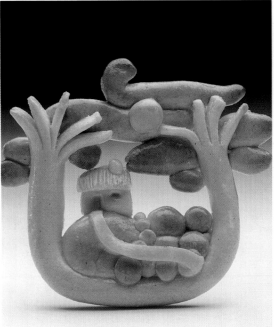

BASKETS

Use an ovenproof bowl as your base and cover it completely with foil. Turn the bowl upside down and position strips and decorations of dough over it. Cook until the dough is partially dry, remove from the oven and take off the bowl and the foil. Return the basket to the oven until it is completely dry.

CHOOSE WIDE-MOUTHED ITEMS AS YOUR SHAPES

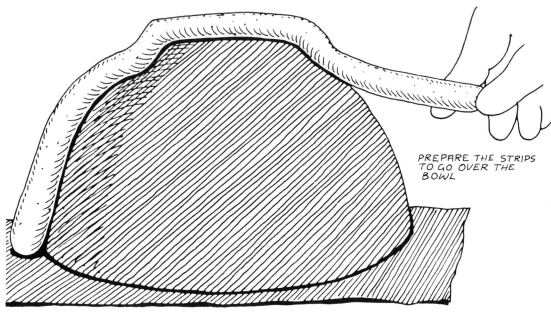

PREPARE THE STRIPS TO GO OVER THE BOWL

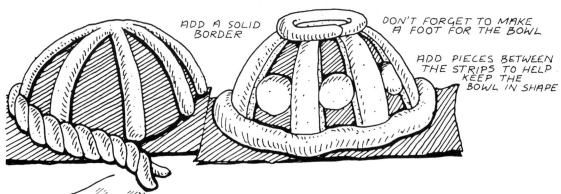

ADD A SOLID BORDER

DON'T FORGET TO MAKE A FOOT FOR THE BOWL

ADD PIECES BETWEEN THE STRIPS TO HELP KEEP THE BOWL IN SHAPE

REMOVE THE BOWL FROM THE HALF-COOKED DOUGH AS SOON AS YOU CAN

- BE CAREFUL, IT WILL BE HOT

FINISH COOKING WITHOUT THE BOWL OR FOIL

Place motifs upside-down between the strips, making sure that you don't leave large gaps. Use separate pieces of dough to give an impression of solidity.

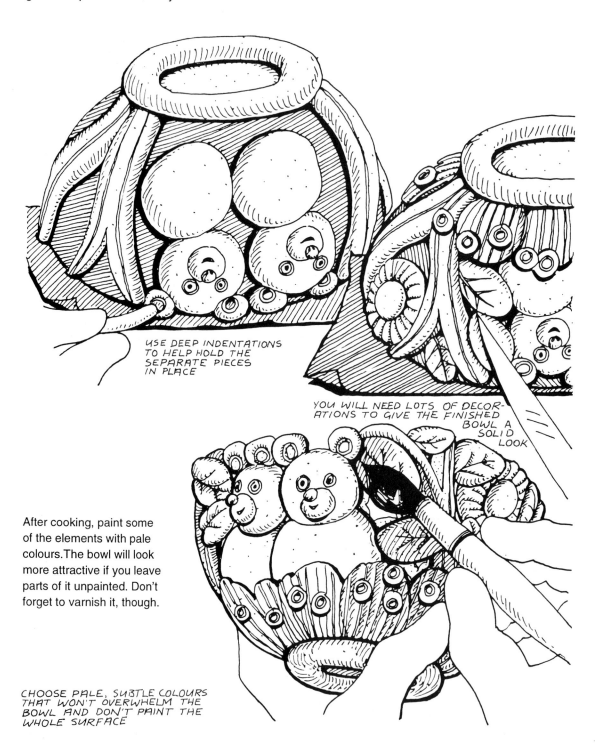

USE DEEP INDENTATIONS
TO HELP HOLD THE
SEPARATE PIECES
IN PLACE

YOU WILL NEED LOTS OF DECOR-
ATIONS TO GIVE THE FINISHED
BOWL A
SOLID
LOOK

After cooking, paint some of the elements with pale colours. The bowl will look more attractive if you leave parts of it unpainted. Don't forget to varnish it, though.

CHOOSE PALE, SUBTLE COLOURS
THAT WON'T OVERWHELM THE
BOWL AND DON'T PAINT THE
WHOLE SURFACE

WREATHS

These little pieces cook very quickly, so keep your eye on them while they cook. They are made from circles, sausages, plaits and wheels – and they can be made into almost any shape you wish.

ROCKING HORSE

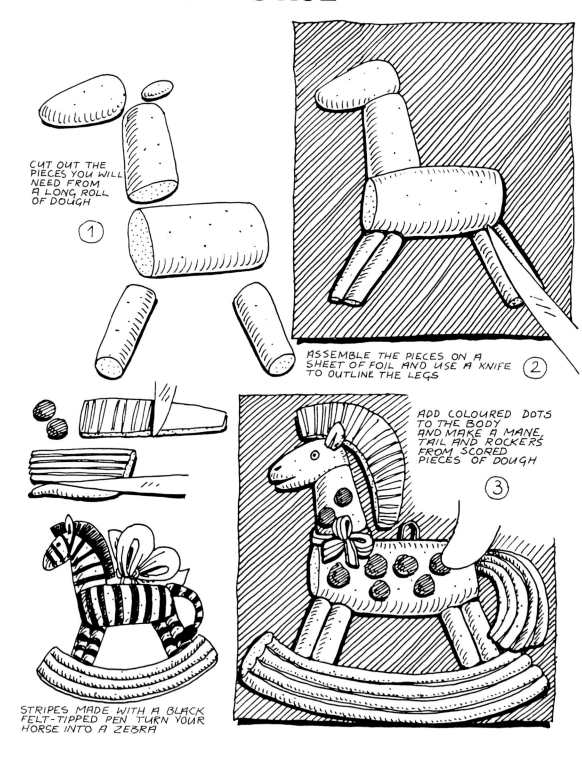

CUT OUT THE PIECES YOU WILL NEED FROM A LONG ROLL OF DOUGH

①

ASSEMBLE THE PIECES ON A SHEET OF FOIL AND USE A KNIFE TO OUTLINE THE LEGS ②

ADD COLOURED DOTS TO THE BODY AND MAKE A MANE, TAIL AND ROCKERS FROM SCORED PIECES OF DOUGH

③

STRIPES MADE WITH A BLACK FELT-TIPPED PEN TURN YOUR HORSE INTO A ZEBRA

MAKING
COSTUMES

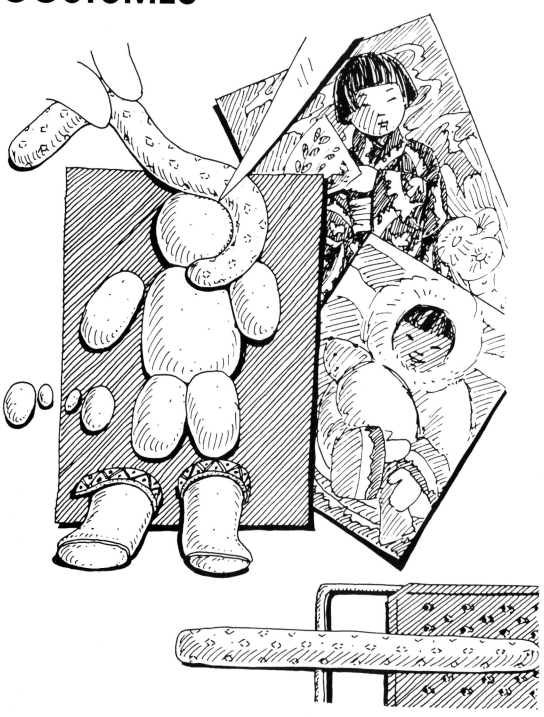

Look at illustrations in books to get some ideas, then use your imagination to transform them into dough motifs.

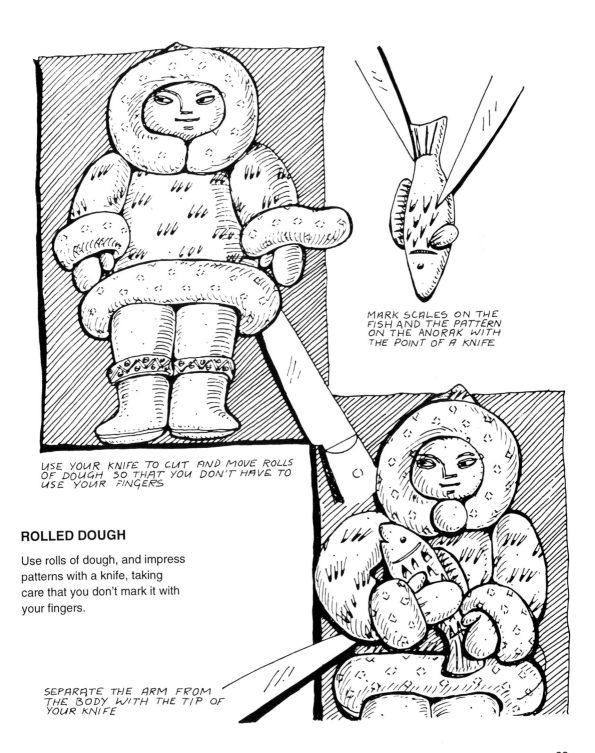

MARK SCALES ON THE FISH AND THE PATTERN ON THE ANORAK WITH THE POINT OF A KNIFE

USE YOUR KNIFE TO CUT AND MOVE ROLLS OF DOUGH SO THAT YOU DON'T HAVE TO USE YOUR FINGERS

ROLLED DOUGH

Use rolls of dough, and impress patterns with a knife, taking care that you don't mark it with your fingers.

SEPARATE THE ARM FROM THE BODY WITH THE TIP OF YOUR KNIFE

PLEATED AND FOLDED DOUGH

Roll out some dough as thinly as you can, then use it like cloth.
Remember, it will tear easily, so handle it carefully.

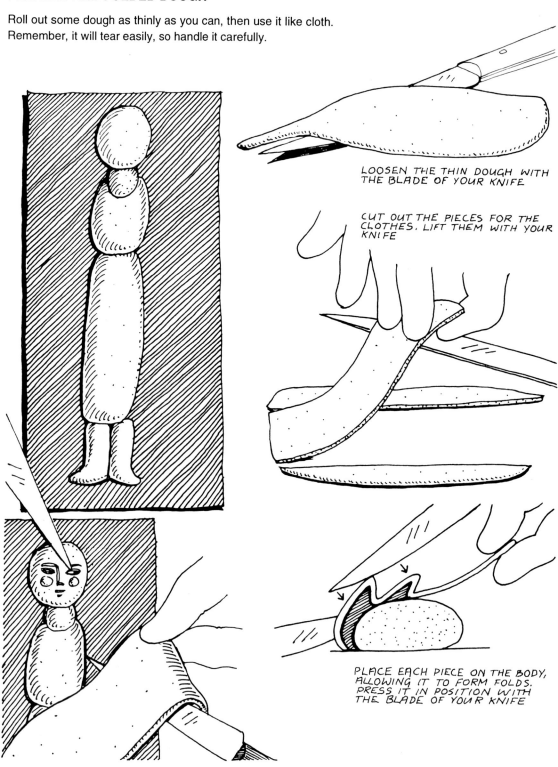

LOOSEN THE THIN DOUGH WITH THE BLADE OF YOUR KNIFE

CUT OUT THE PIECES FOR THE CLOTHES. LIFT THEM WITH YOUR KNIFE

PLACE EACH PIECE ON THE BODY, ALLOWING IT TO FORM FOLDS. PRESS IT IN POSITION WITH THE BLADE OF YOUR KNIFE

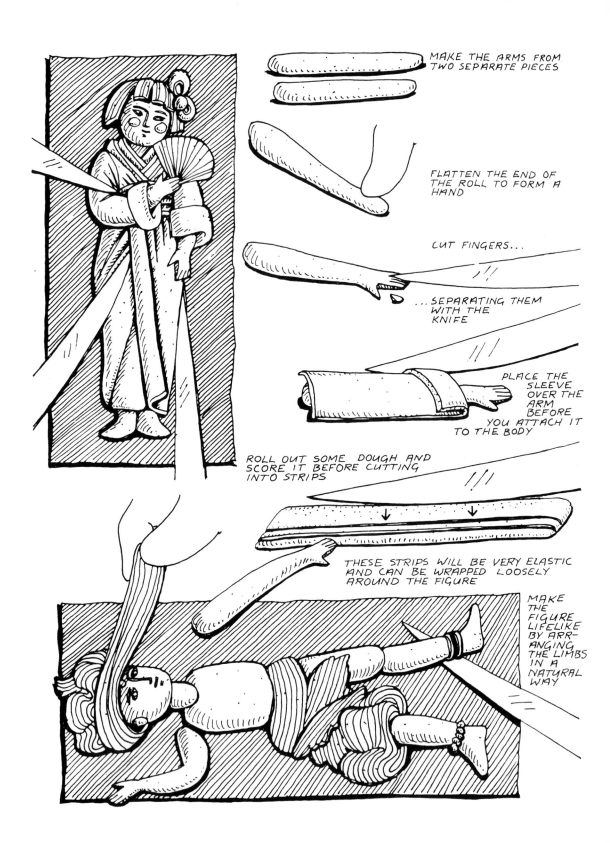

MAKE THE ARMS FROM TWO SEPARATE PIECES

FLATTEN THE END OF THE ROLL TO FORM A HAND

CUT FINGERS...

...SEPARATING THEM WITH THE KNIFE

PLACE THE SLEEVE OVER THE ARM BEFORE YOU ATTACH IT TO THE BODY

ROLL OUT SOME DOUGH AND SCORE IT BEFORE CUTTING INTO STRIPS

THESE STRIPS WILL BE VERY ELASTIC AND CAN BE WRAPPED LOOSELY AROUND THE FIGURE

MAKE THE FIGURE LIFELIKE BY ARRANGING THE LIMBS IN A NATURAL WAY

BIRTHDAY TREE

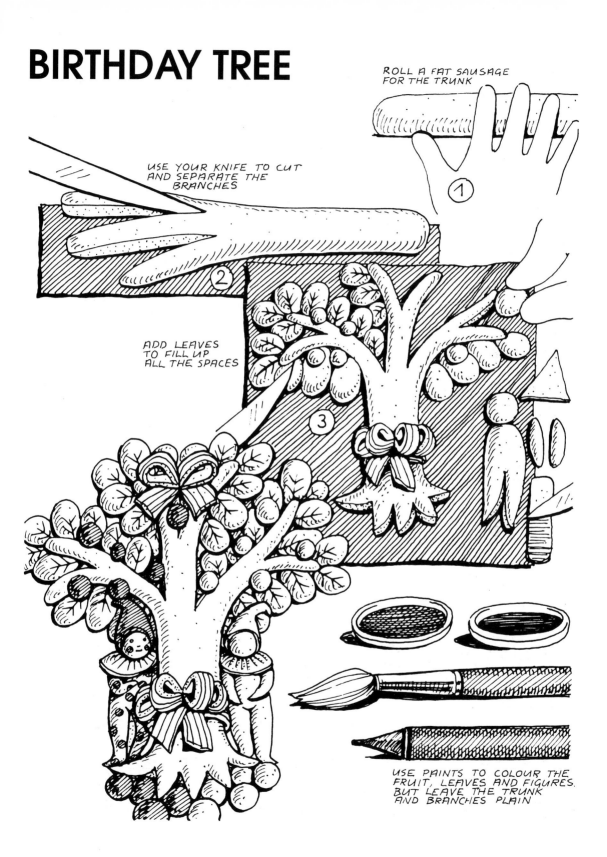

ROLL A FAT SAUSAGE FOR THE TRUNK

①

USE YOUR KNIFE TO CUT AND SEPARATE THE BRANCHES

②

ADD LEAVES TO FILL UP ALL THE SPACES

③

USE PAINTS TO COLOUR THE FRUIT, LEAVES AND FIGURES. BUT LEAVE THE TRUNK AND BRANCHES PLAIN

PASTA SHAPES

Large pasta shapes (*cannelloni* or *millerighe*, from delicatessen shops) are ideal for hollow objects. If they are hard to get, try cardboard cylinders for the objects here and on page 46.

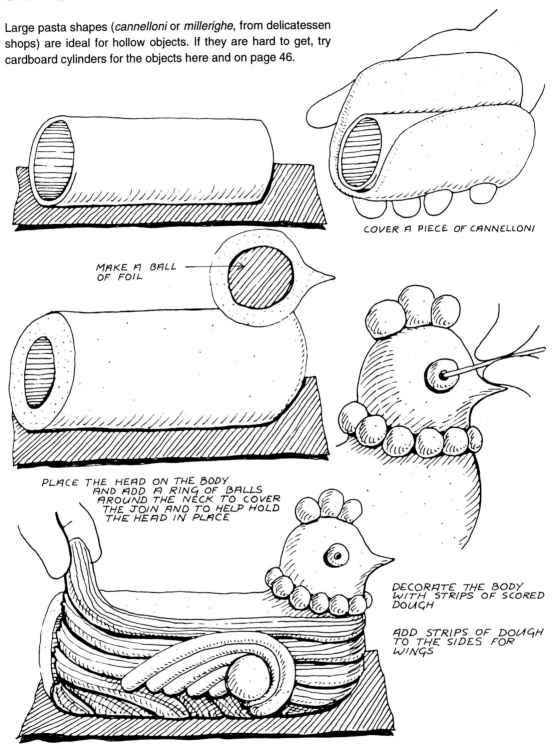

COVER A PIECE OF CANNELLONI

MAKE A BALL OF FOIL

PLACE THE HEAD ON THE BODY AND ADD A RING OF BALLS AROUND THE NECK TO COVER THE JOIN AND TO HELP HOLD THE HEAD IN PLACE

DECORATE THE BODY WITH STRIPS OF SCORED DOUGH

ADD STRIPS OF DOUGH TO THE SIDES FOR WINGS

Delicate pieces should be baked at a low temperature – no more than 120°C/225°F/gas mark$\frac{1}{2}$. Keep the amount of dough in each figure to a minimum – use a ball of foil inside a head, for example – and make sure that the whole figure is completely dry. Large balls or thick rolls of dough will cook first on the outside while the centre remains damp. This will prevent the varnish from adhering properly and will eventually cause the figure to disintegrate.

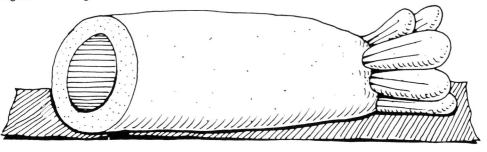

NEVER LEAVE A LARGE SURFACE UNDECORATED. ALWAYS COVER IT WITH SMALL PIECES OF DOUGH – THE FISH, FOR EXAMPLE, SHOULD BE COVERED WITH TINY CIRCLES TO REPRESENT THE SCALES

THESE ARE JUST A FEW OF THE MANY HOLLOW MODELS THAT YOU CAN MAKE IF YOU USE A SHAPE

CONTENTS